£5.45

Welcome To THE BEANO BOOK

Now let's take a look at the folks in this book,
I'm sure there's a lot who you'll know.
We'll name you a few of this top laughter crew,
And then we'll be on with the show.

First there's a boy who seems to enjoy
Annoying his parents and teachers.
So please welcome DENNIS, our top rated menace,
You'll see him in lots of great features.

And not far behind I'm sure that you'll find
His tough dogs called GNASHER and GNIPPER.
If they can't get bones, they chew great big stones
Or maybe poor Dad's bedroom slipper.

The next one you'll meet may look small and sweet,
But don't let her cuteness deceive.
'Cos IVY'S big plan's to be bad as she can —
It's something she's bound to achieve.

BILLY WHIZZ is so fast — one blink and he's past.
This fellow can certainly zoom.
So quickly he ran, this speedy young man
Once set off a loud sonic BOOM.

The BASH STREET KIDS' class won't let a day pass
Without causing Teacher despair.
To make up for this, Toots gave him a kiss
And a large spiky plant on his chair.

One little man is a great football fan.
Yes, BALL BOY'S a real soccer liker.
Even at night, when off goes the light,
He dreams that's he's Britain's top striker.

THE THREE BEARS, by gosh, just love scoffing nosh.
They guzzle far more than they should.
At one famous feast, they ate ten tons at least,
And still found some room for their pud.

Could name you some more you're sure to adore.
I'd go on for ages and ages.
It's going to be great — I know you can't wait,
So, read on, get turning those pages!

It's a BEAR'S LIFE
1.
HIYA, READERS! LET ME SHOW YOU HOW WE POLAR BEARS SPEND A DAY —
3.
— THEN I WASH MY HAIR 'N' GO —
MPOO
— TO THE CUBS! —
4.

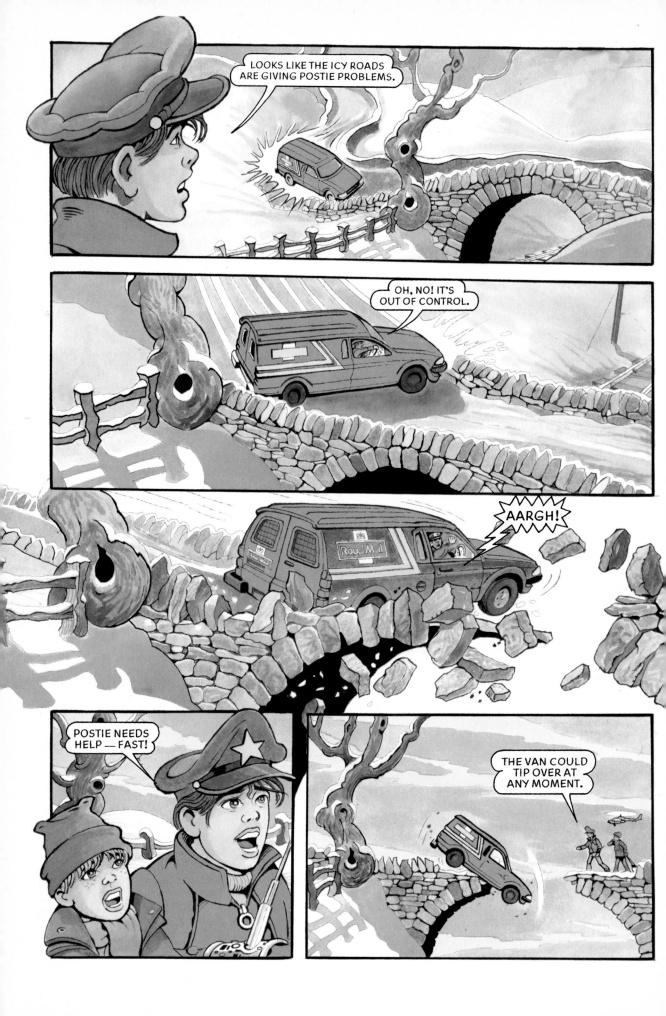

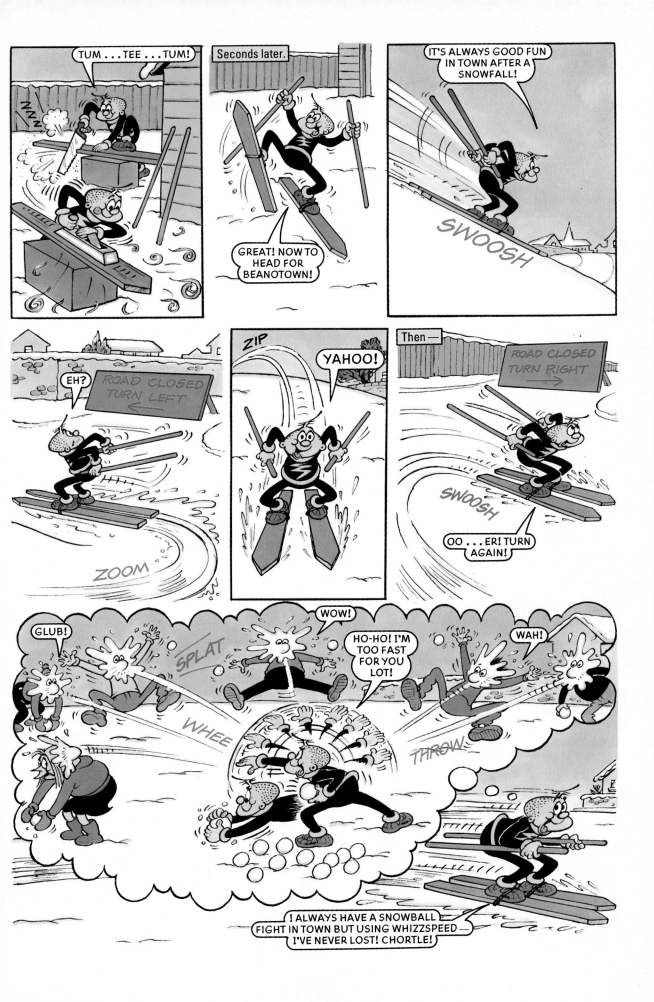

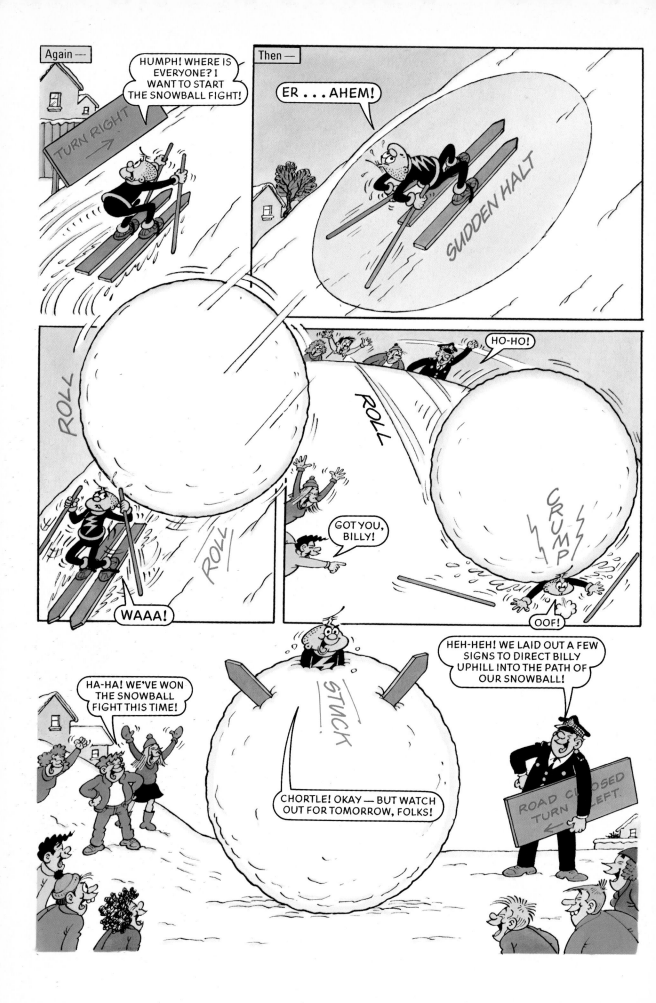

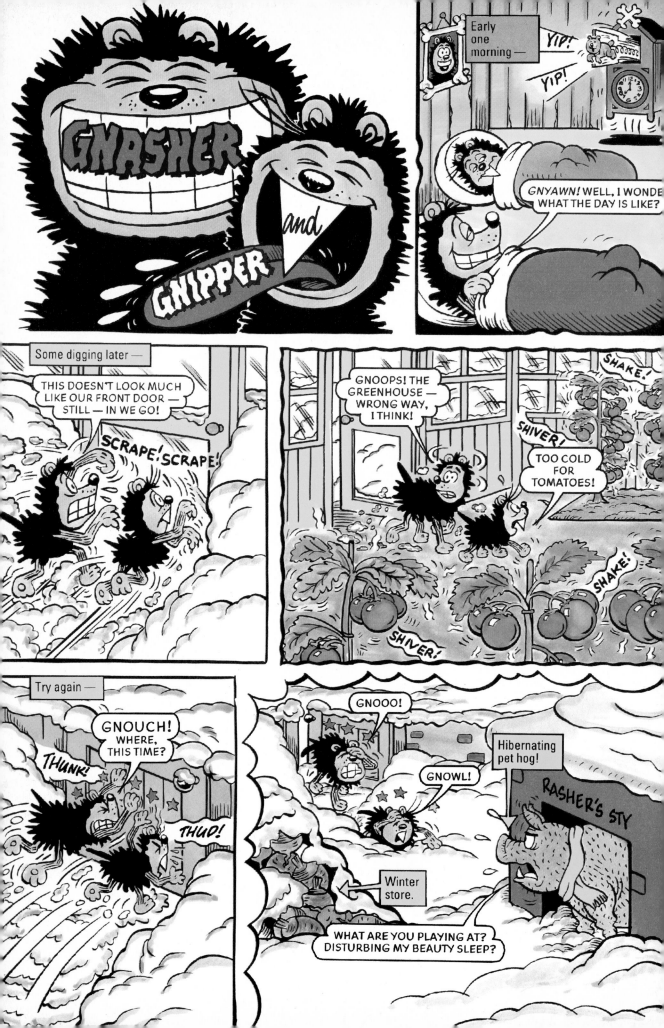

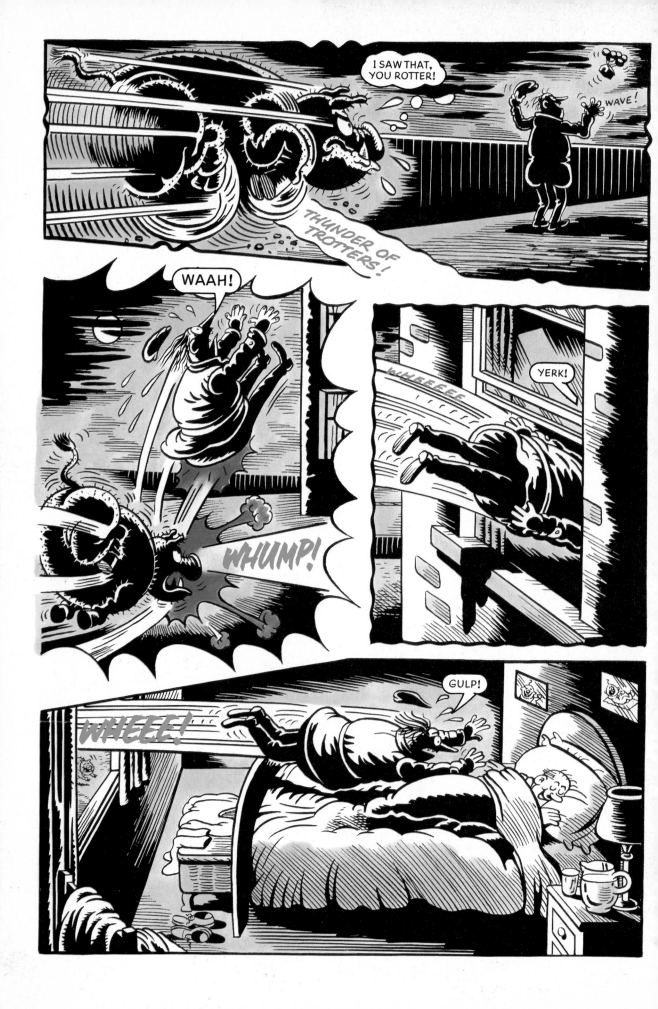

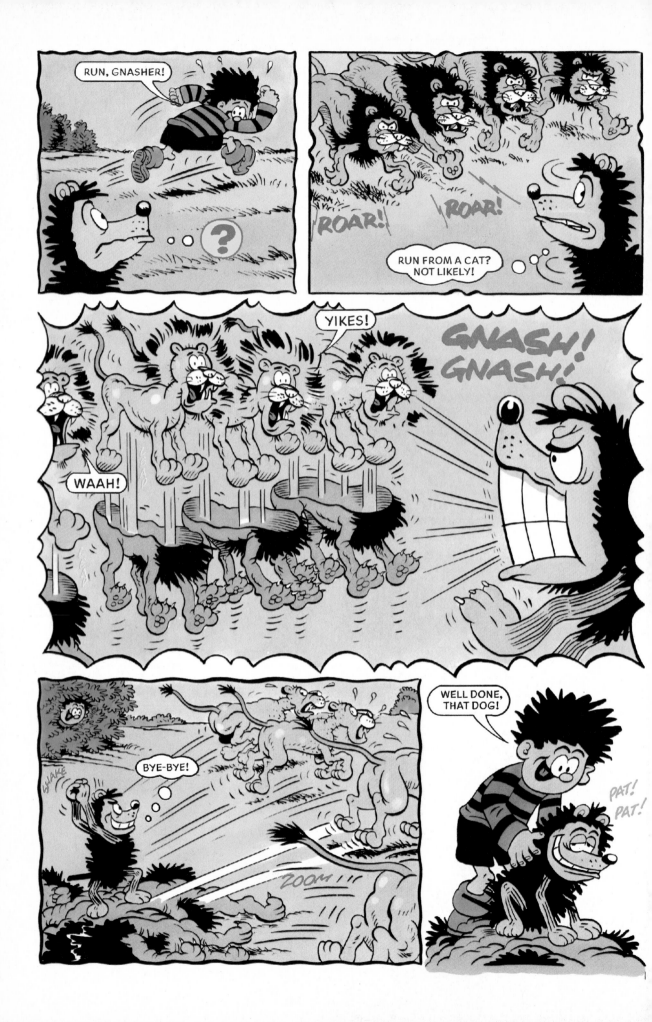

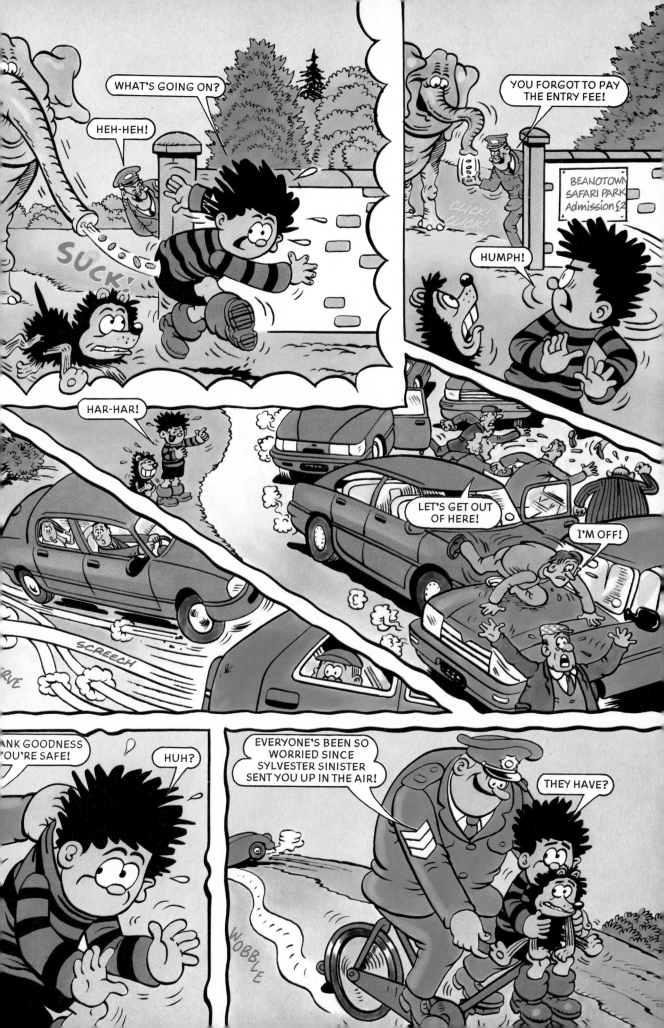

Joke by Karla Laird, Glasgow.

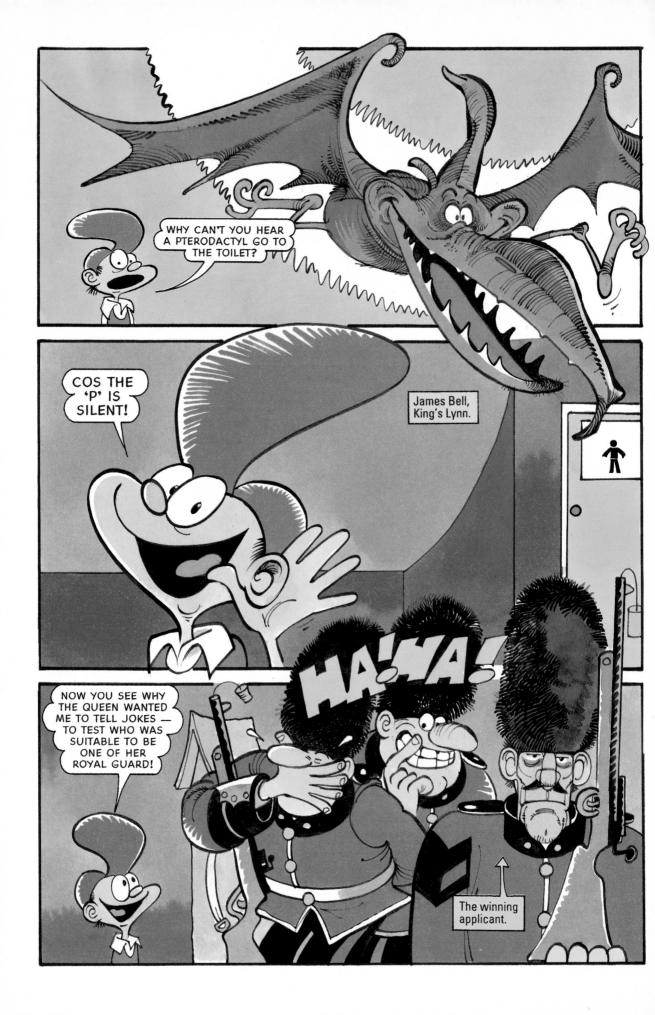

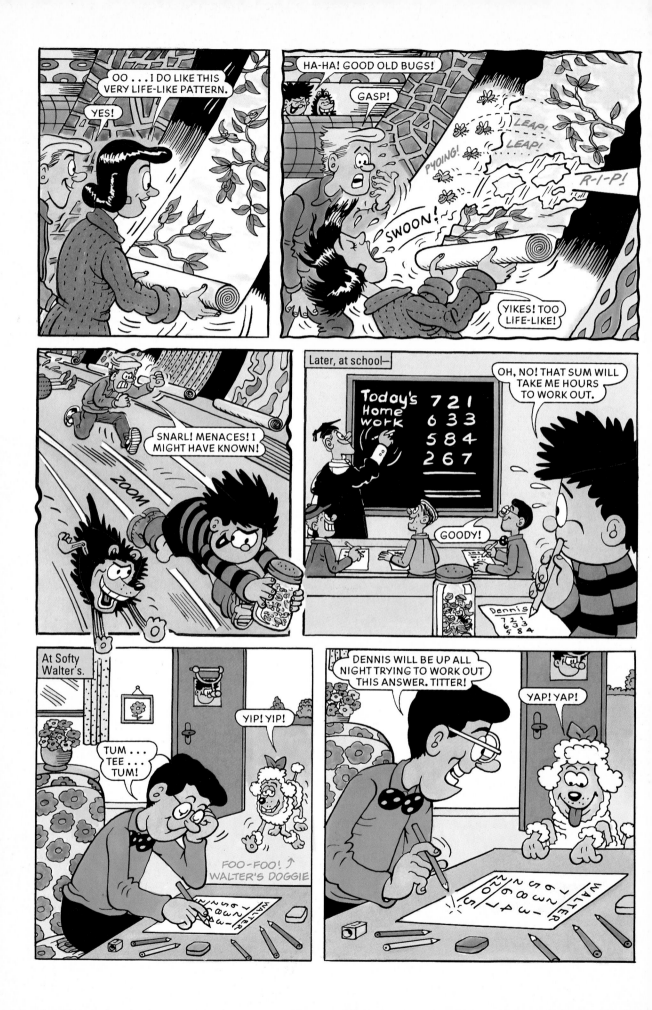

The Eyes Have It!

CAN you match up each pair of Dennis's eyes with their correct definition?

Definitions —

Yipes! What a shock!

Softies! Grr!

ZZZZ!

Chinese food for tea

Tennis

Mum asked me to peel some onions

Homework!

Too much T.V?

Acrobatics

Who let off that flash gun?

Late night

Pogo-stick!

The Bash Street Kids in:-

"CASTLE HASSLE"

"**W**OW! Look at that ancient ruin!" said Smiffy. "Stop insulting me and let's get on with this school trip!" replied Teacher, as their bus arrived in the grounds of Blithering Castle.

"What-ho! Pip-pip! Come in! Don't stand on ceremony!" said Sir Stanley Blithering as he invited Teacher and the kids into his castle home. At that moment a cat screamed. "I told you not to stand on ceremony," Sir Stanley bleated. "Sorry!" replied Fatty sheepishly, removing his foot from the tail of Ceremony, Sir Stanley's black and white (or should that be black and blue?) pet moggy.

"Thank you for letting us look round your fabulous home," crawled Teacher. He was on his hands and knees as Danny had tied his shoe laces together.

"Not at all, old bean! My pleasure!" said Sir Stanley waspishly (Wilbur, one of Sid's pet wasps, was stinging his nose at the time).

"Let's go into the portrait gallery," continued his Lordship in a muffled tone — the bandage he had put on his nose had caught on his prominent front teeth.

The wind whistled down the long corridor as they headed into the portrait gallery. "Down the Long Corridor" is not a well known tune so nobody joined in.

"That must be one of your relatives — he looks just like you!" said the short-sighted 'Erbert. "Actually, that's a hatstand," explained Sir Stanley, "though now you mention it, it DOES look rather like Aunt Hilda!"

Everyone laughed like a pack of hyenas in a tickling stick factory.

The laughing soon stopped, however, as Sir Stanley began a long-winded description of his family tree. All the kids (except 'Erbert) could see the tree for themselves through an open window and were not impressed. "It's just an old oak tree," said Wilfrid woodenly.

It soon became obvious that the kids were bored. "WE'RE BORED!" screamed Plug at the top of his voice. "We're very bored!" said Toots at the foot of her voice. "We're very, very bored!" said Spotty in the middle of his voice.

His Lordship kept on speaking in a distinctive, high-pitched nasal twang. This was matched by the distinctive, high-pitched elastic twang of Danny's catapult as he let loose an aged tomato at the gibbering Lord.

"I say, old fruit!" said Sir Stanley perceptively. The tomato splattered against his fizzog. Teacher was red with embarrassment and his Lordship was red with tomato. "How can I ever apologise?" said Teacher in a sorry state.

Sir Stanley was beside himself with rage. "I must be seeing double!" remarked 'Erbert. The enraged Lord then pressed a concealed button that was hidden from view.

A trapdoor opened up and Teacher and the kids plummetted downwards. Down, down, down they fell for what seemed like an eternity but was really just a very, very long time. The kids landed softly on the cold stone floor (actually they landed on Teacher).

"He's trapped us in a bottle dungeon!" Teacher cried — the kids were still on top of him. Teacher was right, there were lemonade bottles chained to all the walls and wine bottles on racks.

"We've got to get out of here!" said Teacher in a high-pitched whine that only dogs could hear. Danny had an idea. "I've had an idea!" he said. "Smiffy — pretend you're a dog!" barked Danny. "Woof!" replied Smiffy.

"Now dig for a bone!" continued Danny, brightly. "What are you on about?" said the rest, dully.

WAG!

WAG!

POP

POP

POP POP

At that moment Smiffy started digging into the floor, using his hard head as a shovel. "Great idea!" said Plug, who believed in calling a spade a spade.

In less time than it takes a lisping man with laryngitis to say: "Twenty-two tickets to Timbuctoo", Smiffy had dug a tunnel out of the castle and led everyone to safety. "Good boy!" Teacher patted his head and gave him a dog biscuit.

At that point a loud rumbling noise reached their ears (it reached Plug's ears first as they were the biggest). "Must be my tum — I need food!" said Fatty greedily, before eating the rest of Teacher's dog biscuits. Fatty ate so many he developed a shiny coat and a cold, wet nose, but still the rumbling continued.

"Look at that!" said Danny, pointing a finger and three toes at Blithering Castle. The castle was crumbling to the ground before their very eyes, noses and teeth.

"Smiffy's tunnel must have brought the foundations to breaking point!" Teacher snapped.

When the dust cleared away, after a particularly loud biscuit-fuelled burp from Fatty, the furious figure of Sir Stanley Blithering could be seen hopping mad among the ruins.

"Ho-ho! Looks like his ancestral pile has been reduced to an ancestral pile of RUBBLE!" laughed Plug. Everyone joined in the laughter as they headed home — except Fatty and Smiffy who just barked and wagged their bottoms.

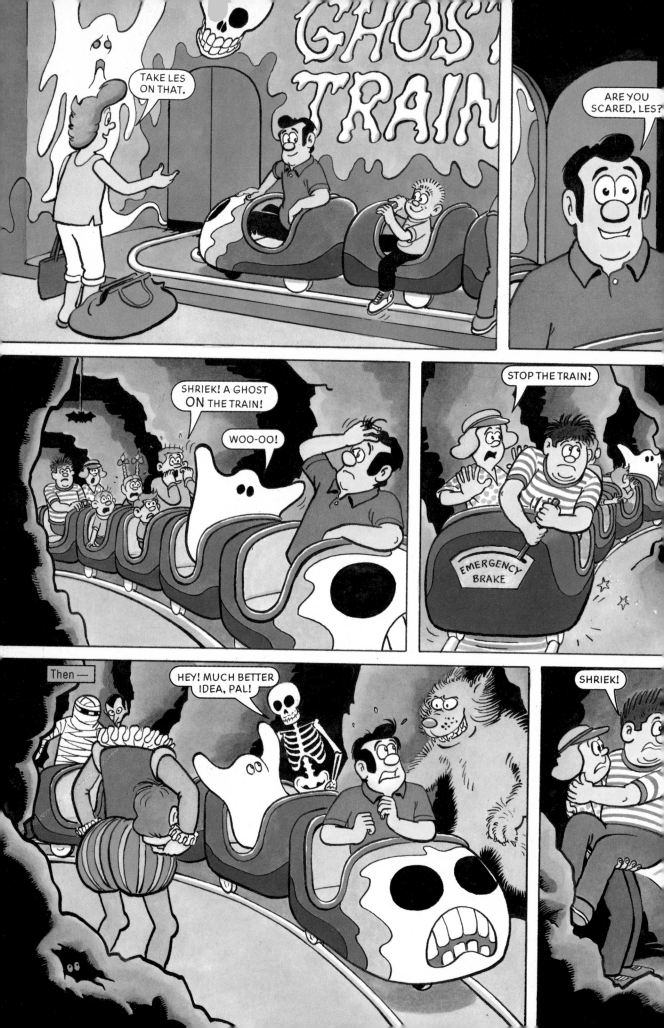